Stars of the Sea

MATAPEAKE ELEMENTARY SCHOOL

By Allan Fowler

Consultants

Linda Cornwell, Coordinator of School Quality
and Professional Improvement
Indiana State Teachers Association

Jan Jenner, Ph.D.

Children's Press®
A Division of Grolier Publishing
New York   London   Hong Kong   Sydney
Danbury, Connecticut

Visit Children's Press® on the Internet at:
http://publishing.grolier.com

Designer: Herman Adler Design Group
Photo Researcher: Caroline Anderson
The photo on the cover of this book shows a Dawson's sun sea star.

Library of Congress Cataloging–in–Publication Data

Fowler, Allan.
    Stars of the sea / by Allan Fowler.
      p. cm. — (Rookie read-about science)
    Includes index.
    Summary: Describes the physical characteristics, habitats, and behavior
of sea stars, also known as starfishes.
    ISBN 0-516-21214-1 (lib. bdg.)   0-516-27057-5 (pbk.)
    1. Starfishes—Juvenile literature. [1. Starfishes.] I. Titles.
II. Series.
QL384.A8F74   2000   98-52941
593.9'3—dc21   CIP
                                               AC

©2000 Children's Press®
A Division of Grolier Publishing Co., Inc.
All rights reserved. Published simultaneously in Canada
Printed in the United States of America
    3 4 5 6 7 8 9 10 R 09 08 07 06 05 04 03 02

Where do you look for stars? In the sky, at night?

You can also find stars on the beach and in the ocean.

They are living stars called sea stars or starfishes.

Gulf sea star

Most sea stars have five
arms and are shaped
like a five-pointed star.

Gulf sea star

Purple sun sea star

Others may have more arms.

Sea stars are usually between 8 and 12 inches across.

Their arms can stretch out more than 24 inches.

9

Cobalt sea star

Sea stars may be yellow, orange, red, blue, purple, or brown.

Sea stars use feet to crawl along the ocean bottom.

Their feet are tiny tubes on the underside of their arms.

Tube feet on the arm of a sea star

The mouth of this sea star is black and white.

A sea star has a mouth on the bottom of its body.

A sea star eats by pushing
its stomach out through
its mouth.

Then it gobbles up fish.

This bat sea star is eating two fish.

18

If a sea star's arm gets cut off, an amazing thing can happen.

The arm can grow into a new sea star!

There are many kinds
of sea stars.

A brittle star has long
arms and a round body.

Brittle star

Orange-footed sea cucumber

Sea cucumbers (KYOO-kuhm-burz) are related to sea stars. They look a lot like the cucumbers we eat.

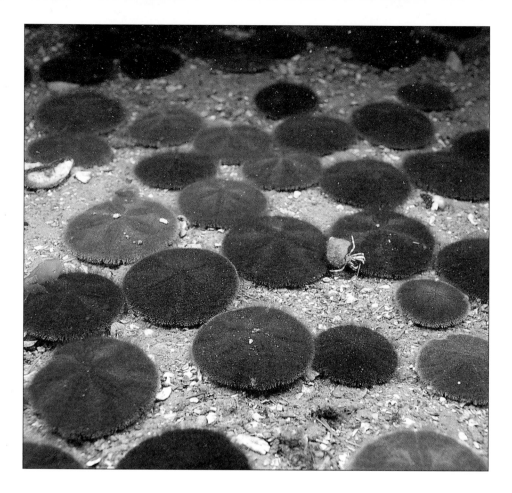

Sand dollars are also
related to sea stars.

Can you see the star on
the top of this sand dollar?

26

An ocean beach is a great place to find sea stars.

But in the water these
stars really shine!

Marble sea star

Words You Know

brittle star

mouth

sand dollar

sea cucumber

sea star

stomach

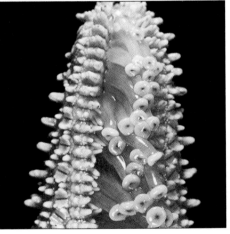

tube feet

31

Index

About the Author

Allan Fowler is a freelance writer with a background in advertising.
Born in New York, he now lives in Chicago and enjoys traveling.

Photo Credits

©: Photo Researchers: 21, 30 top (L. Newman & A. Flowers), 10
(E. R. Degginger), 3 (Allan Morton & Dennis Milon/SPL), 5, 31 bottom
(Gregory G. Dimijian, M.D.), 7, 24 (Andrew J. Martinez), 17 (Tom McHugh/
Steinhart Aquarium), 9 (Mark Newman), 25, 30 bottom (Dan Sudia), 18
(Stuart Westmorland); Visuals Unlimited: cover, 26 (Gerald & Buff Corsi),
13 (John D. Cunningham), 14 (Michael DeMocker), 29 (Alex Kerstitch),
22, 31 top (Gustav W. Verderber); Wildlife Collection: 6 (Chris Huss).